BODY RAGS

BODY RAGS

BY GALWAY KINNELL

1968
HOUGHTON MIFFLIN COMPANY BOSTON

FIRST PRINTING   W

To Inés

ACKNOWLEDGMENTS

Certain of the poems in this volume have previously appeared in various books and magazines, as follows:

Choice: Mango, Testament of the Thief
Colorado State Review: Getting the Mail
The Hudson Review: The Porcupine
The Minor Bird: The Falls
The Nation: Last Songs, Night in the Forest
The New Yorker: The Fossils, La Bagarède
The Paris Review: Another Night in the Ruins
Poetry: The Last River (under the title "The Mystic River"), The Correspondence School Instructor Says Goodbye to His Poetry Students, The Poem, In the Anse Galet Valley, How Many Nights, In the Farmhouse
A Poetry Reading Against the Vietnam War: Vapor Trail Reflected in the Frog Pond
The Sixties: Going Home by Last Light, The Bear

CONTENTS

PART I

ANOTHER NIGHT IN THE RUINS   3

LOST LOVES   5

GETTING THE MAIL   6

VAPOR TRAIL REFLECTED IN THE FROG POND   7

THE FOSSILS   9

THE BURN   11

ONE WHO USED TO BEAT HIS WAY   13

THE FLY   14

THE FALLS   15

MANGO   16

IN THE ANSE GALET VALLEY   17

LA BAGARÈDE   18

NIGHT IN THE FOREST   19

GOING HOME BY LAST LIGHT   20

HOW MANY NIGHTS   22

LAST SONGS   23

IN THE FARMHOUSE   24

THE CORRESPONDENCE SCHOOL INSTRUCTOR SAYS
GOODBYE TO HIS POETRY STUDENTS   25

THE POEM   27

PART II

THE LAST RIVER 33

PART III

TESTAMENT OF THE THIEF 51

THE PORCUPINE 56

THE BEAR 60

PART ONE

ANOTHER NIGHT
IN THE RUINS

1

In the evening
haze darkening on the hills,
purple
of the eternal, a last bird
crosses over, '*flop flop*',
adoring
only the instant.

2

Nine years ago,
in a plane that rumbled all night
above the Atlantic,
I could see, lit up
by lightning bolts jumping out of it,
a thunderhead formed like the face
of my brother, looking nostalgically down
on blue,
lightning-flashed moments of the Atlantic.

3

He used to tell me,
"What good is the day?
On some hill of despair
the bonfire
you kindle can light the great sky —
though it's true, of course, to make it burn
you have to throw yourself in . . ."

3

4

Wind tears itself hollow
in the eaves of my ruins, ghost-flute
of snowdrifts
that build out there in the dark:
upside-down
ravines into which night sweeps
our torn wings, our ink-spattered feathers.

5

I listen.
I hear nothing. Only
the cow, the cow
of nothingness, mooing
down the bones.

6

Is that a
rooster? He
thrashes in the snow
for a grain. Finds
it. Rips
it into
flames. Flaps. Crows.
Flames
bursting out of his brow.

7

How many nights must it take
one such as me to learn
that we aren't, after all, made
from that bird which flies out of its ashes,
that for a man
as he goes up in flames, his one work
is
to open himself, to *be*
the flames?

LOST LOVES

1

On ashes of old volcanoes
I lie dreaming,
baking
the deathward flesh in the sun,

and dream I can hear
a door, far away,
banging softly in the wind:

Mole Street. Quai-aux-Fleurs. Françoise.
Greta. "After Lunch" by Po Chu-I.
"The Sunflower" by Blake.

2

And yet I can rejoice
that everything changes, that
we go from life
into life,

and enter ourselves
quaking
like the tadpole, his time come, tumbling toward the
    slime.

GETTING THE MAIL

I walk back
toward the frog pond, carrying
the one letter, a few wavy lines
crossing the stamp: tongue-streaks
from the glue
and spittle beneath: my sign.

The frogs'
eyes bulge toward the visible, suddenly
an alderfly glitters past, declining
to die: her third giant step
into the world.

And touching
the name stretched over the letter
like a blindfold, I wonder,
what did *getting warm* used to mean? And tear

open the words,
to the far-off, serene
groans of a cow
a farmer is milking in the August dusk
and the Kyrie of a chainsaw drifting down off Wheelock
    Mountain.

VAPOR TRAIL
REFLECTED IN THE FROG POND

1

The old watch: their
thick eyes
puff and foreclose by the moon. The young, heads
trailed by the beginnings of necks,
shiver,
in the guarantee they shall be bodies.

In the frog pond
the vapor trail of a SAC bomber creeps,

I hear its drone, drifting, high up
in immaculate ozone.

2

And I hear,
coming over the hills, America singing,
her varied carols I hear:
crack of deputies' rifles practicing their aim on stray dogs
    at night,
sput of cattleprod,
TV groaning at the smells of the human body,
curses of the soldier as he poisons, burns, grinds, and stabs
the rice of the world,
with open mouth, crying strong, hysterical curses.

3

And by rice paddies in Asia
bones
wearing a few shadows
walk down a dirt road, smashed
bloodsuckers on their heel, knowing
the flesh a man throws down in the sunshine
dogs shall eat
and the flesh that is upthrown in the air
shall be seized by birds,
shoulder blades smooth, unmarked by old feather-holes,
hands rivered
by blue, erratic wanderings of the blood,
eyes crinkled up
as they gaze up at the drifting sun that gives us our lives,
seed dazzled over the footbattered blaze of the earth.

THE FOSSILS

1

In the cliff over the frog pond
I clawed in the flagmarl and stones,
crushed up
lumps half grease half dust:
atrypas came out,
lophophyllidiums casting shadows,
corals bandaged in wrinkles,
wing-shaped allorismas,
sea-lily disks . . .
which did not molder into dust
but held.

Night rose up
in black smoke, making me
blind. My fingertips rubbed
smooth on my brain, I knelt in the dark, cracking
the emptiness,
poking spirifers into flying black dust,
letting sylvan remains slither through my fingers,
whiffing the glacial roses,
feeling the pure absence of the ephemera . . .

And shall
I have touched
the ornithosuchus, whose wings
try, not to evade earth, but to press closer to it?

2

While Bill Gratwick flapped, pranced
and called the dances,
light-headed
as a lizard on hind legs I sashayed
with Sylvia, of the woods, as woodwinds
flared and crackled in the leaves,
Sylph-ia, too, of that breeze
for whom even the salamander rekindles wings;
and I danced the eighteenth-century shoulder-rub
with Lucy,
my shoulder blades starting to glitter
on hers as we turned, sailbacks
in laired and changing dance,
our faces smudged with light from the fingertips of the
    ages.

3

Outside
in dark fields
I pressed the coiled
ribs of a fingerprint to a stone,
first light in the flesh.

Over the least fossil
day breaks in gold, frankincense, and myrrh.

THE BURN

Twelve years ago I came here
to wander across burnt land,
I had only begun to know
the kind of pain others endure,
I was too full of sorrows.
Now, on the dirt road
that winds beside the Kilchis River
to the sea, saplings
on all the hills, I go deep
into the first forest of Douglas firs
shimmering out of prehistory,
a strange shine up where the tops
shut out the sky, whose roots
feed in the waters of the rainbow trout.
And here, at my feet, in the grain
of a burnt log opened by a riverfall,
the clear
swirls of the creation. At the
San Francisco airport, Charlotte,
where yesterday my arms
died around you like old snakeskins, the puffed
needletracks on your arms
marked how the veins wander.
I see you walking like a somnambulist
through a poppy field, blind
as myself on this dirt road, tiny
flowers brightening about you,
the skills of fire, of fanning
the blossoms until they die,

perfected; only the power to nurture
and make whole, only love,
impossible. The mouth of the river.
On these beaches
the sea throws itself down, in flames.

ONE WHO USED TO
BEAT HIS WAY

Down the street of warehouses,
each with
its redlighted shaftway,
its Corinthian columns,
its bum crapped out on the stoop,
he staggers, among
wraiths that steam up out of manhole covers
and crimesheets skidding from the past.

He gets a backed-up
mouthful of vomit-cut liquor, mumbles, "Thanks God,"
and regulps it. And
behind him the continent glimmers, the wild land
crossed by the *Flying Crow*
that changed her crew at Shreveport,
the *Redball* and the *Dixie Flyer*, that went on through,
the *Big 80*
that quilled her whistles to make blues on the Delta.
"Everybody's eating everybody, and nobody
gives a shit where they bite,"
the old timer growls, poking the jungle fire . . .
"Bible-ranters, bulls, hicks, systems, scissor-bills . . ."

And he who used
to beat his way hauls himself down
into his wino-niche, where he has left his small possessions,
a killed bottle,
a streambed of piss groping down the dry stone.

THE FLY

1

The fly
I've just brushed
from my face keeps buzzing
about me, flesh-
eater
starved for the soul.

One day I may learn to suffer
his mizzling, sporadic stroll over eyelid and cheek,
even seize on his burnt
singing with love.

2

The bee is beautiful.
She is the fleur-de-lys in the flesh.
She has a tuft of the sun on her back.
She brings sexual love to the narcissus flower.
She sings of fulfillment only
and stings and dies.
And everything she ever touches
is opening! opening!

And yet we say our last goodbye
to the fly last,
the flesh-fly last,
the absolute last,
the naked dirty reality of him last.

THE FALLS

The elemental murmur
as they plunge, *croal, croal,*
and *haish, haish,* over
the ledges,
through stepless wheels
and bare axles, down between
sawmills that have
buckled and slid sideways to their knees . . .

When I fall I would fall to my sounding . . .
the lowly,
unchanged, stillic, rainbowed sounding
of the Barton River Falls.

MANGO

1

It opens in three: yellow-gold
as dawn
on the mudwalls of Hafez' garden,
on a seagull mewing for the light,
on the belly of a Chinese dancing-girl,

austere,
smacking of turpentine,
a bit stringy, like the mortal flesh.

2

Under
the mango limbs
overfilled with flesh,
a few crones squat by the whitening sea,
clapping, chorusing of love.

IN THE ANSE GALET VALLEY

1

Clouds
rise by twos out of the jungle, cross
under the moon, and sink
into
the peak called Font-des-Serpents.

I remember the child's game:
angel's wings,
laid-open scallop shell,
gowpen overspilling milled grain,
two moles feeling their way through the light,
myself and . . .

2

A straw torch
flickers
far off among the trees,
of a nightfisherman
wading upstream clubbing the fishes.

The fer-de-lances
writhe in black winding-skins,
the grail-bearers go down, dissolving.
What question could I have asked, the wafer-
moon
gnawed already at its death-edge?

LA BAGARÈDE

1

I take the dogs into
town and buy chèvre and a bâtard.
Back at La Bagarède I eat
this little meal in the dusk
and sit a long time, until

the Swan grows visible, trailing
her indicated wings down the horizon,
and Orion
begins to stalk the last nights of the summer.

2

The black
water I gulp from the spring
hits my brain at the root. And
I can hear
the giant, dark blooms of sunflowers
crackling open. And in the sky
the seventh
of the Sisters, she who hid herself
for shame
at having loved one who dies, is shining.

NIGHT IN THE FOREST

1

A woman
sleeps next to me on the earth. A strand
of hair flows
from her cocoon sleeping bag, touching
the ground hesitantly, as if thinking
to take root.

2

I can hear
a mountain brook
and somewhere blood winding
down its ancient labyrinths. And
a few feet away
charred stick-ends surround
a bit of ashes, where burnt-out, vanished flames
absently
waver, absently leap.

GOING HOME BY LAST LIGHT

1

Redheaded by last light,
with high-stepped, illusionist amble
I walk toward the white room
where she is waiting,
past
pimentos,
red cabbages,
tomatoes flickering in their bins,
past melons, past mushrooms and onions.

2

Those swarms
of Mayflies that used to rise
at the Vermont threshold, "imagos"
thrown up for a day,
their mouths shriveling closed,
their wings,
their sexual parts, newborn and perfect . . .

3

For several minutes
two mosquitos have been making love
on top of this poem,
changing positions, swooning, even they,
their thighs
fragile as a baby's hairs, knowing
the ecstasy.

4
A day!
The wings of the earth
lift and fall
to the groans, the cold, savage thumpings of a heart.

HOW MANY NIGHTS

How many nights
have I lain in terror,
O Creator Spirit, Maker of night and day,

only to walk out
the next morning over the frozen world
hearing under the creaking of snow
faint, peaceful breaths . . .
snake,
bear, earthworm, ant . . .

and above me
a wild crow crying *'yaw yaw yaw'*
from a branch nothing cried from ever in my life.

LAST SONGS

1

What do they sing, the last birds
coasting down the twilight,
banking
across woods filled with darkness, their
frayed wings
curved on the world like a lover's arms
which form, night after night, in sleep,
an irremediable absence?

2

Silence. Ashes
in the grate. Whatever it is
that keeps us from heaven,
sloth, wrath, greed, fear, could we only
reinvent it on earth
as song.

IN THE FARMHOUSE

1

Eaves moan,
clapboards flap,

behind me the potbellied
stove
Ironside #120, rusty, cracked,
rips thick chunks of birchwood
into fire.

2

Soon it will be spring,
again the vanishing of the snows,

and tonight
I sit up late, mouthing
the sounds that would be words
in this flimsy jew's-harp of a farmhouse
in the wind
rattling on the twelve lights of blackness.

THE CORRESPONDENCE SCHOOL
INSTRUCTOR SAYS GOODBYE
TO HIS POETRY STUDENTS

Goodbye, lady in Bangor, who sent me
snapshots of yourself, after definitely hinting
you were beautiful; goodbye,
Miami Beach urologist, who enclosed plain
brown envelopes for the return of your *very*
"Clinical Sonnets"; goodbye, manufacturer
of brassieres on the Coast, whose eclogues
give the fullest treatment in literature yet
to the sagging breast motif; goodbye, you in San Quentin,
who wrote, "Being German my hero is Hitler,"
instead of "Sincerely yours," at the end of long,
neat-scripted letters demolishing
the pre-Raphaelites:

I swear to you, it was just my way
of cheering myself up, as I licked
the stamped, self-addressed envelopes,
the game I had
of trying to guess which one of you, this time,
had poisoned his glue. I did care.
I did read each poem entire.
I did say what I thought was the truth
in the mildest words I knew. And now,
in this poem, or chopped prose, not any better,
I realize, than those troubled lines
I kept sending back to you,
I have to say I am relieved it is over:
at the end I could feel only pity
for that urge toward more life

your poems kept smothering in words, the smell
of which, days later, would tingle
in your nostrils as new, God-given impulses
to write.

Goodbye,
you who are, for me, the postmarks again
of shattered towns — Xenia, Burnt Cabins, Hornell —
their loneliness
given away in poems, only their solitude kept.

THE POEM

1

On this hill crossed
by the last birds, a sprinkling
of soil covers up the rocks
with green, as
the face
drifts on a skull scratched with glaciers.

The poem too
is a palimpsest, streaked
with erasures, smelling
of departure and burnt stone.

2

The full moon
slides from the clouds, the trees'
graves all lie out at their feet:

the leaf
shaped tongue
of the new born and the dying
quivers, and no one interprets it.

3

Where is "The Apocalypse of Lamech"?
Where is the "Iliupersis"?
Where is the "Khavadhaynamagh"?
Where is the "Rommant du Pet au Deable"?
Where is "The Book of the Lion"?

Where is the servantose of the sixty girls of Florence?
Where are the small poems Li Po folded into boats and
      pushed out on the river?
Where are the snows that fell in these graves?

4

On this hillside strewn with
fistbones unclasping for the first time from the pistol and
      club,
fatalist wishbones,
funnybones gone up in laughing gas,
astralagi from which the butterflies have flown,
innominate bones,
sacrums the eucharist-platters of kites,
and here and there a luz-bone dead of non-resurrection,

we hunt
the wild hummingbird
who once loved nesting in these
pokeweed-sprouting, pismired
ribcages dumped down all over the place.

5

On a branch
in the morning light, at the tip
of an icicle, the letter C
comes into being — trembles,
to drop, or to cling?

Suddenly a roman
carapace glitters all over it. Look:

6

Here is a fern-leaf binding *utter* to the image of *illume*,
here is a lightning-split fir the lines down its good side
      becoming whitmanesque and free,

here is *unfulfilled* reflected as *mellifica* along the feather
   of a crow,
here is a hound chasing his bitch in trochaic dimeter
   brachycatalectic,
here are the pits where the tongue-bone is hurled at its
   desolate cry,
here are my own clothes composing *emptiness* in khaskura,
here is a fly convulsing down the poisoned labyrinth of
   this poem,
here is an armful of last-year's-snows.

7
The moment
in the late night, when baby birds
closed in dark wings almost stir, and objects
on the page grow suddenly
heavy, hugged
by a rush of strange gravity:

the surgery of the funeral
and of the funeral oration, the absence
in the speech I will have left in the world
of

8
Where are "The Onions"
that I saw swollen with tears on a grocery shelf
in 1948?

brong ding plang ching of a spike
driven crazy on a locust
post.

PART TWO

THE LAST RIVER

1

When I cross
on the high, back-reared ferry boat
all burnished brass and laboring pistons
and look at the little tugs and sticklighters
and the great ships from foreign lands
and wave to a deckhand gawking at the new world
of sugar cane and shanties and junked cars
and see a girl by the ferry rail,
the curve the breeze makes down her thigh,
and the green waves lighting up . . .
the cell-block
door crawls open and they fling us a pimp.

2

The lights dim,
the dirty jokes die out.

Rumble of trailertrucks
on Louisiana 1 . . . I think
of the rides
back from the courthouse in Amite,
down the canyon between
faces smiling from the billboards,
the car filled
with black men who tried to register to vote . . .
Tickfaw . . . Independence . . . Albany . . .

Moan of

a riverboat creeping
upstream. . . yap and screech
of police dogs
attacking the police in their dreams.

3

Under the blue flasher
and the siren's wail, I gazed out,
I remember, at anything,
anything at all of the world . . .
surreal spittoon . . .
glow of EAT . . .
fresh-hit carcass . . . cat . . . coon . . .
polecat . . .

and then lightning flashed,
path strung out a moment across the storm,
bolt of love even made of hellfire
between any strange life and any strange life,
blazed
for those who shudder in their beds
hearing a siren's wail
fading down a dead-ridden highway at night . . .
thump . . . armadillo . . . thump . . . dog . . .

4

Somebody wakes,
he's got himself a "nightcrawler" — one of those
jokes that come to you in your sleep —
about girls who have "cross-bones"
and can't, consequently,
be entered . . . An argument flares up
on whether there is, or is not,
a way to circumvent the cross-bone . . .
"Sheee-it! Sheee-it!" the copbeater cries,
and the carthief says, "Jeee-ziz! Jeee-ziz!"
"All right boys," the pimp puts in from time to time,

"What say? Let's get a little fucking sleep."

5

I turn on the iron bunk . . .
One day in Ponchatoula
when the IC from Chicago crept
into the weeds of the Deep South, and stopped,
I thought I saw three
of my kinsmen from the North
in the drinking car, boozing their way
down to New Orleans,
putting themselves across,
selling themselves,
dishing up soft soap,
plump, manicured, shit-eating, opulent, razor-sharp . . .

Then the train
lurched and pushed on, carrying them off,
Yankee . . . equalitarian . . .
grease in the palm of their golden aspirations.

6

When I think America consists
only of billboards that smile,
I think of my friends
out there,
from Plaquemine or Point Coupee,
who go from shanty to shanty
in the dust,
fighting to keep empty
the space in their breast, to trudge
through the dust for nothing,
nothing at all,

the dust
suddenly changed
into pollen of sunflowers, giving light at their feet.

7

The carthief's face,
oddly childish as he sleeps,
reminds me now of Jesus — a Jesus
I saw on a Negro funeral parlor calendar,
blue-eyed, rosy-cheeked, milky and soft . . .

I remember his beautiful speech of the old days . . .
those prayers, funeral orations, anthems,
war songs, and — actual poems! some of them
as beautiful as,
for example, "Wall Kill," "Terre Haute,"
"Stillwater," "Alcatraz" . . . under its name
each more escapeproof,
more supersecure,
more insane than the last,
liberty, said Shelley, being
"brightest in dungeons."

The carthief moans in his sleep, his face
now like a cat's.

8

Through the crisscross
of bars at the tiny window
I could see the swallows
that were darting in the last light,
late-flying creatures that surpass us in plain view . . .
bits of blurred flesh . . .
wavy lines . . .

Nothing's there now but a few stars
brightening
under the ice-winds of the emptiness . . .

Isn't it strange
that all love, all granting of respect,

has no face for its passing expressions but yours,
Death?

9

I hear now
the saddest of songs, the humming
the dew makes
as it dries from the garlic leaf.

A new night
and the dew will come back again,
for so many men
the chance to live as men
does not ever come.

10

I remember
the ancient ex-convict
who teaches voter-registration
in his shanty under the levee, standing
in the sun on the dirt road . . .
a crepe myrtle tree,
a passion flower,
a butterfly . . .

In the green, blistered sewer,
among beer cans, weeds, plastic flowers,
a few lumps of excrement, winged
with green flies.

The dust on the road
swirls up into little wing-shapes, that blow off,
the road made of dust goes down . . .

He smiles,
the air brightens as though ashes

of lightning bolts had been scattered through it.

What is it that makes the human face,
bit of secret,
lighted flesh, open up the earth?

11

A girl and I are lying
on the grass of the levee. Two
birds whirr overhead. We lie close,
as if having waked
in bodies of glory.

And putting on again
its skin of light, the river
bends into view. We watch it, rising
between the levees, flooding for the sky,
and hear it,
a hundred feet down, pressing its long weight
deeper into the world.

The birds have gone,
we wander slowly homeward, lost
in the history of every step . . .

12

I am a child
and I am lying face-down
by the Ten Mile River, one half mud
and one half piss, that runs
between the Seekonk Woods
and the red mills of Pawtucket
with their thousand windows and one smokestack,
breathing the burnt odor
of old rocks,
watching a bug breaking itself up,
holding

to my eye a bleached catfish
skull I turned up in the grass,
inside it, in the pit of light, a cross,

hearing the hornpout sounding
their horns mournfully deep inside the river.

13

Across
the dreamlit waters pushes
the flag-topped Plaquemine ferry,
and midway between shore and shore
it sounds its horn, and catfishes
of the Mississippi caterwaul and nose over,
heavy-skulled,
into the flinty, night-smelling depths.

14

All my life, of rivers
I hear
the longing cries, rut-roar
of shifted wind
on the gongs of beaten water . . .

the Ten Mile of Hornpout,
the Drac hissing in its bed of sand,
the Ruknabad crossed by ghosts of nightingales,
the Passumpsic bursting down its length in spring,
the East River of Fishes, the more haunting for not
      having had a past either,
and this Mississippi coursing down now through the silt of
      all its days,
and the Tangipahoa, snake-cracked, lifting with a little
      rush from the hills and going out in thick, under-
      nourished greenery.

15

Was there some last
fling at grace in those eddies, some swirl
back toward sweet scraping, out there
where an Illinois cornstalk
drifts, turning the hours,
and the grinned skull of a boy?

The burning fodder dowses down,
seeking the snagged
bodies of the water-buried,
bits
of sainfoin sopped in fire, snuffed from below

down the flesh-dark Tallahatchie,
the bone-colored Pearl.

16

I wrench
a tassel of moss from a limb
to be my lightning-besom and sweep
the mists from the way.

Ahead of me a boy is singing,

    didn't I ramble
    I rambled
    I rambled all around
    in and out the town
    I rambled
    I rambled till the butcher cut me down . . .

He comes out of the mist,
he tells me his name is Henry David,
he takes my hand and leads me over the plain of crushed
    asphodels.

17

Who's this
at water's edge,
oar in hand, kneeling beside
his pirogue of blue stern . . .
no nose left,
no hair,
no teeth,
little points of flame for eyes,
limbs tied on with knots and rags?

"Let's go," I say, a big
salty wafer of spit in my mouth.

We step in
to the threshold groan, the pressurized
bayou water squirts in
at the seams, we oar out
on water brown-green
in the patches free of scum, nothing on all sides
but the old, quiet, curious diet of green,
alligatorwood,
swamp gum, tupelo, liquid amber,
live oak chrisomed in air-eating moss,
cypress grief-shaped among her failed roots . . .

18

Down here the air's
so thick with American radio-waves,
with our bare ears we can pick up
the groggy, backcountry announcers
drawling their pitch and hardsell:
to old men forgotten under armies of roaches,
to babies with houseflies for lips and eyelashes,
to young men without future puking up present and past,
to recidivists sentenced deep into the hereafter,

to wineheads only a rusty penknife and self-loathing for
    arms,
to hillbilly boys breaking out in sweat at the anti-sweat
    ads,
to . . .
        "Listen!" says Henry David.
"Sheee-it! Sheee-it!" a cupreous-
throated copbeater's chattering far-off in the trees.

19

On the shore four souls
cry out in pain, one lashed
by red suspenders to an
ever-revolving wheel, one with
red patches on the seat of his pants
shrieking while paunchy vultures
stab and gobble at his bourbon-squirting liver,
one pushing uphill
his own belly puffed up with the blood-money
he extorted on earth, that crashes back
and crushes him, one
standing up to his neck
in the vomit he caused the living to puke . . .

"Southern politicians," Henry David says,
"Yonder, in Junkie's Hollow,
you'll find Northern ones . . ." I see one,
formerly mayor of a great city, as he draws
a needle from his arm, black
blood, bits
of black testicle dribble from the puncture.

20

A man comes lurching
toward me with big mirrors for eyes,
"Sammich!" he cries and doubles up in laughter.
I remember him at once, from ten years ago,

in Chicago, on a Sunday
in a park on the death-scented South Side,
in the days before my own life had even begun,
when full of strut and happiness
this person came up and cried, "Sammich!"
and now he says, "A fight,
I was makin' the scene and the fuzz
did blast my fuckin' ass off." He laughs.
He is also crying. He shrinks back. "Hey,"
he calls, "thanks for that sammich that day . . .
fat white bastard . . ."

21

We come to a crowd, hornets
in their hair, worms in their feet.
"They weren't for anything or against anything,"
Henry David says, "they looked out
for themselves."

Three men trot beside us,
peddling bits of their flesh,
dishing up soft screams,
plump, manicured, shit-eating, opulent . . .

Underfoot a man
with stars on his shoulders
grapples in the slime with his Secretary of Profit.
I kick it off him and he gets up.
"I stood above all partisan squabbles,"
he howls,
flashes the grin
that so loved itself it sold itself to the whole world,
and plunges into the slime, throttling his Secretary of
    Sanctimony.

22

We come to robed
figures bunched on their knees,
meek eyes rolled up. By twitches
in their throats we gather they're alive.
"Rafel mai ameck zabi almi," they intone together.

Down on all fours, like a cat
at his saucer of fresh cream, their leader,
blue-eyed, rosy-cheeked, milky and soft, laps
with big tongue at a mirror.

23

Off to one side there's a man
signing restrictive covenants with his fingernails
on a blackboard. "That one,"
says my guide, "was
well-meaning; he believed
in equality and supported the good causes;
he got a shock, when he found out
this place is run by logicians . . ."
Hearing us talk, the man half turns . . .
"Come on," I say, sweating, for I know him.

24

We pass
victims of the taste for blood
who were hanged by the mob
just as the law was about to hang them,
we pass victims of justice
who were hanged by the mob for having got
stays of execution, executive pardons, or fair trials,
we pass victims of sexual dread
who cover, as we approach, the scabs at their crotches.

Here and there we see
"unknown persons"

killed for "unknown reasons"
at the hands of "persons unknown" . . .

25
We come to a river
where many thousands kneel, sucking up
its cloudy water
in a kind of frenzy . . .

"What river is it?" I ask.
"The Mystic River," Henry David says,
"the Healing Stream free to all
that flows from Calvary's Mountain . . . the liquor
that makes you forget . . ."

"And what's over there,
on the far shore?" "That?"
he says, "that's Camp Ground . . ."

I turn to see the police whipping
a child who refuses to be born,
she shrieks
and scrambles for the riverbank
and stands
singing in a floating, gospel wail,
"Oh Death, he is a little man . . ."

"What's it like in Camp Ground?" I ask.

But in the mist I only hear,

   I rambled
   in and out the town
   didn't I ramble
   I rambled . . .

26

My brain rids itself of light,
at last it goes out completely,
slowly
slowly
a tiny cell far within it
lights up:

a man of noble face
sits on the iron bunk, wiping
a pile of knifeblades clean
in the rags of his body.
My old hero. Should I be surprised?

"Hard to wash off . . .
buffalo blood . . . Indian blood . . ." he mutters,
at each swipe singing, *"mein herz! mein herz!"*

"Why you," I ask him,
"You who, in your life, loathed our crimes?"

"Seeking love . . . love
without human blood in it,
that leaps above
men and women, flesh and erections,
which I thought I had found
in a Massachusetts gravel bank one spring . . .
seeking love . . .
failing to know I only loved
my purity . . . *mein herz! mein* fucking *herz!"*

"Hey," somebody
from another cellblock shouts, "What say?
Sleep . . . sleep . . ."

The light goes out. In the darkness
a letter for the blind
arrives in my stunned hands.

Did I come all this way only for this, only
to feel out the world-braille of my complicity,
only to choke down these last poison wafers?

For Galway alone.
I send you my mortality.
Which leans out from itself, to spit on itself.
Which you would not touch.
All you have known.

27
On one bank
of the last river stands
a black man, on the other
a white man, on the water between
a man of no color,
body of beryl,
face of lightning,
eyes lamps of wildfire,
arms and feet of polished brass.

There will come an agony upon you
beyond any
this nation has known;
and at that time thy people,
given intelligence, given imagination, given love,
        given . . .

Here his voice falters, he drops
to his knees, he is
falling to pieces,
no nose left,
no hair,
no teeth,
limbs dangling from prayer-knots and rags,

waiting by the grief-tree
of the last river.

PART THREE

TESTAMENT OF THE THIEF

1

Under the forked
thief-shadow lunging by the breeze,
a coolie sits, resting,
having lugged
a sack of earth over the earth:
shirt open,
legs spread,
head lolled to one side,
sweat-trickles,
plants,
tiny animals,
stylized all over him.

2

And on good terms
with the claustrophobic pewk-worm,
the louse,
the nerve-wracked flea,

a beggar has sprawled
all day on the ground — who can say
whether from laziness or love? — while waters

rustle in their blue grooves, and birds
ask,
    'koja? koja?'

3
"This fellow is a colonel,
the degenerate next to him is a cop,
the scarecrow in the coma is a highschool principal,
the one dyed yellow
is chief of the narcotics squad,
that meatsack smokes to bring his weight down,
the squat one
puffing tragically is a poet
broken by longing to be Minister of Finance.

"Me? I just fix
their pipes, and hang on, stabbing
my poor portion of the world
with skinny assbones, waiting for my favorite to come,
a mean little boy
who is my most glorious punishment yet.

"Oh once
I regretted my life,
the only regret I have left, the only
poignant one, is the way
they soak you for opium.

"Listen,
I may be washed up,
but when you think of me, mull over
this proverb, will you? If
the cat had wings
he would gobble up every bird in the sky."

4
The wild rose dies,
the hollyhock dies,
the poppy does not come back,
the moth preens herself all season long
for the one, carnal moment.

And yet a rose
has tossed the corpse its perfume.
that
that bloated snout could catch it proves
the body, too,
has had its springs in paradise.

5
A breeze off the bazaar,
lotus,
wild olive,
gum tragacanth,
indigo, musk,
burnt seed of wild rue,
gillyflower . . .

Under the breeze, in the dusk,
the poor cluster at tiny
pushcarts of fire, eating
boiled beets,
gut,
tongue,
testicle,
cheeks, forehead, little feet.

Down this street
the thief used to ramble, picking his way
in his pajamas of derangement,
on just
this spot, after a meal, he would sleep,
the earth drawing
all his bones down close upon it.

Stop a moment, on his bones' dents,
stand without moving, listen
to the ordinary people

as they pass. They do not sing
of what is gone or to come, they sing of
the old testaments of their lives,
the little meals,
the airs,
the streets of our time.

6

"*Item,* to the opium master
dying in paradise: this nose,
in working disorder,
crazed
for the poison fumes of the real.

"*Item,* to the beggar
dumped on blue stone, gasping
as, one after one, girl friends
of his youth hallucinate his nap:
these bones, their
iron faithfulness to loss.

"*Item,* to the coolie
who trudges over the earth bearing
earth on his backbones,
whose skeleton
shall howl for its dust like any other
on the bitter slopes of the creation:
this
ultimate ruckus on the groan-meat."

7

Item, to the pewk-worm
who lives all his life in our flesh,
nuzzling along
through fat and lean, skinny and soft,
gnawing himself a peephole when lost, in buttock or
        cheek,

whom you can drag forth
only by winding him up on a matchstick
a quarter turn a day for the rest of your days:
this map of my innards.

THE PORCUPINE

1

Fatted
on herbs, swollen on crabapples,
puffed up on bast and phloem, ballooned
on willow flowers, poplar catkins, first
leafs of aspen and larch,
the porcupine
drags and bounces his last meal through ice,
mud, roses and goldenrod, into the stubbly high fields.

2

In character
he resembles us in seven ways:
he puts his mark on outhouses,
he alchemizes by moonlight,
he shits on the run,
he uses his tail for climbing,
he chuckles softly to himself when scared,
he's overcrowded if there's more than one of him per five
        acres,
his eyes have their own inner redness.

3

Digger of
goings across floors, of hesitations
at thresholds, of
handprints of dread
at doorpost or window jamb, he would
gouge the world

empty of us, hack and crater
it
until it is nothing, if that
could rinse it of all our sweat and pathos.

Adorer of ax
handles aflow with grain, of arms
of Morris chairs, of hand
crafted objects
steeped in the juice of fingertips,
of surfaces wetted down
with fist grease and elbow oil,
of clothespins that have
grabbed our body-rags by underarm and crotch . . .

Unimpressed — bored —
by the whirl of the stars, by *these*
he's astonished, ultra-
Rilkean angel!

for whom the true
portion of the sweetness of earth
is one of those bottom-heavy, glittering, saccadic
bits
of salt water that splash down
the haunted ravines of a human face.

4
A farmer shot a porcupine three times
as it dozed on a tree limb. On
the way down it tore open its belly
on a broken
branch, hooked its gut,
and went on falling. On the ground
it sprang to its feet, and
paying out gut heaved

and spartled through a hundred feet of goldenrod
before
the abrupt emptiness.

5

The Avesta
puts porcupine killers
into hell for nine generations, sentencing them
to gnaw out
each other's hearts for the
salts of desire.

I roll
this way and that in the great bed, under
the quilt
that mimics this country of broken farms and woods,
the fatty sheath of the man
melting off,
the self-stabbing coil
of bristles reversing, blossoming outward —
a red-eyed, hard-toothed, arrow-stuck urchin
tossing up mattress feathers,
pricking the
woman beside me until she cries.

6

In my time I have
crouched, quills erected,
Saint
Sebastian of the
scared heart, and been
beat dead with a locust club
on the bare snout.
And fallen from high places
I have fled, have
jogged
over fields of goldenrod,

terrified, seeking home,
and among flowers
I have come to myself empty, the rope
strung out behind me
in the fall sun
suddenly glorified with all my blood.

7
And tonight I think I prowl broken
skulled or vacant as a
sucked egg in the wintry meadow, softly chuckling, blank
template of myself, dragging
a starved belly through the lichflowered acres,
where
burdock looses the arks of its seed
and thistle holds up its lost blooms
and rosebushes in the wind scrape their dead limbs
for the forced-fire
of roses.

THE BEAR

1

In late winter
I sometimes glimpse bits of steam
coming up from
some fault in the old snow
and bend close and see it is lung-colored
and put down my nose
and know
the chilly, enduring odor of bear.

2

I take a wolf's rib and whittle
it sharp at both ends
and coil it up
and freeze it in blubber and place it out
on the fairway of the bears.

And when it has vanished
I move out on the bear tracks,
roaming in circles
until I come to the first, tentative, dark
splash on the earth.

And I set out
running, following the splashes
of blood wandering over the world.
At the cut, gashed resting places
I stop and rest,
at the crawl-marks

where he lay out on his belly
to overpass some stretch of bauchy ice
I lie out
dragging myself forward with bear-knives in my fists.

3
On the third day I begin to starve,
at nightfall I bend down as I knew I would
at a turd sopped in blood,
and hesitate, and pick it up,
and thrust it in my mouth, and gnash it down,
and rise
and go on running.

4
On the seventh day,
living by now on bear blood alone,
I can see his upturned carcass far out ahead, a scraggled,
steamy hulk,
the heavy fur riffling in the wind.

I come up to him
and stare at the narrow-spaced, petty eyes,
the dismayed
face laid back on the shoulder, the nostrils
flared, catching
perhaps the first taint of me as he
died.

I hack
a ravine in his thigh, and eat and drink,
and tear him down his whole length
and open him and climb in
and close him up after me, against the wind,
and sleep.

5

And dream
of lumbering flatfooted
over the tundra,
stabbed twice from within,
splattering a trail behind me,
splattering it out no matter which way I lurch,
no matter which parabola of bear-transcendence,
which dance of solitude I attempt,
which gravity-clutched leap,
which trudge, which groan.

6

Until one day I totter and fall —
fall on this
stomach that has tried so hard to keep up,
to digest the blood as it leaked in,
to break up
and digest the bone itself: and now the breeze
blows over me, blows off
the hideous belches of ill-digested bear blood
and rotted stomach
and the ordinary, wretched odor of bear,

blows across
my sore, lolled tongue a song
or screech, until I think I must rise up
and dance. And I lie still.

7

I awaken I think. Marshlights
reappear, geese
come trailing again up the flyway.
In her ravine under old snow the dam-bear
lies, licking
lumps of smeared fur
and drizzly eyes into shapes

with her tongue. And one
hairy-soled trudge stuck out before me,
the next groaned out,
the next,
the next,
the rest of my days I spend
wandering: wondering
what, anyway,
was that sticky infusion, that rank flavor of blood, that
    poetry, by which I lived?